Get fit for skiing

Exercises that increase your fitness and flexibility so you get the most from your ski trip

Ian D. McMillan

ISBN 1-55850-995-X

Published by Bob Adams, Inc., 260 Center Street, Holbrook MA 02343.

Printed in the United States of America.

Cover photographs courtesty of Berghaus Limited.

Contents

Acknowledgements

Technical adviser: Charles McDade
Photographer: Roy Houston
Model: Graeme Gunn, member of the Drambuie British Alpine
Ski Team

Introduction

It may seem unnecessary to say that the level of fitness any sport demands must conform to that sports' specific requirements, but with skiing the human body has to contend with a rare mixture of balance, strength, endurance, flexibility and skill—a mixed bag of tricks that gives the sport its popular image of fun, falls and frustration.

Skiing is an acquired skill, the learning of which involves the mastery of movement as well as the basic fitness needed to start and continue learning about the skiing experience. This twinning of skills is very important. If a superfit athlete from another sporting discipline were to try skiing for the first time, unschooled in the dynamics of movement, he would, after a couple of hours skiing in a stiff tense position, punish his highly tuned muscles as much as would the unfit, desk-bound pen-pusher. On the other hand, an out-of-condition, overweight ski instructor could probably cruise about all day with apparent ease. The latter could also tackle difficult terrain quite happily, which would intimidate those who have mastered most slopes, but still have neither the physical or mental strength to plunge into the unknown.

Good technique brings freedom, but you are very unlikely to feel the joy of freedom if you're as stiff as a board during the first few days of a ski trip. All too often the majority of skiers go skiing unfit for what lies ahead, prepared only to go through a predictable process—initial enthusiasm, followed by muscular strain, after which the pains ease so that you're approaching some kind of proficiency just when it's time to go home! But what's needed? How do we get fit for skiing when there are so many different kinds of skiing to prepare for?

This book has been prepared with the different requirements of skiers in mind. Not so much to create perfectly conditioned downhillers, but to make everyone more aware of the need for preparation and, consequently, be better prepared and enjoy the sport much more.

Firstly, an overall general level of fitness is of more use to a wide range of skiers, whether beginner or expert, going on his or her first ever or first outing of the season.

Simply putting your back into sitting against the nearest wall is a popularly held misconception of what is involved in ski exercising, and, while this is not completely wasted exercise, it is fairly insignificant if it is not part of a broad-based fitness effort.

One important thing always to remember, however is never go *skiing* to get *fit,* get *fit* to go *skiing.*

So what kind of fitness do the various levels of ski skill require, taking the earlier illustration of the sportsman and the ski instructor into consideration?

Beginners and the first step

The lack of knowledge for the novice is, as in any new sport, a seemingly insurmountable obstacle to any kind of progress. You can be prepared for the unknown by being reasonably fit but, as in any of life's activities, more important is to be fit for the purpose. A help here is first to get a feel for the initial ungainliness of ski hardware, both skis and the rigid plastic ski boots.

First-hand experience is available at any of the artificial or dry ski slopes up and down the country and certainly at the total novice stage an introductory session is more than just a start in seeing and feeling how the skiing learning process and the equipment will affect your physical condition.

Essentially, learning to ski is the acquisition of technical skills that allow you to use ski equipment efficiently and absorb a totally different set of body mechanisms that enable you to feel at home in a new, sloping world. As far as body mechanisms are concerned, it's often a case of re-learning the balancing skills we use in our everyday lives.

Adults find it harder to learn to ski than children, and not just because, as popular myth would have it, they have further to fall. The really important difference is that children are still at the discovery stage of running,

Small children can often find a perfect balance position.

Fig 1: A beginner, tense from struggling to master basic technique.

Fig 2: A ski instructor on a steep slope in perfect balance.

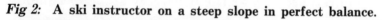

jumping, falling and being totally flexible. Adults, on the other hand, especially those who have given up sports generally, follow familiar and repetitive patterns of everyday life—walking, driving, climbing up and down stairs at a measured rate—and generally do not learn any more about how their bodies move. Overall fitness, therefore, is an important element as it increases the body's flexibility. But there is a qualification to this statement because, try as we might, we can seldom separate the fitness and the technical elements, whether the learner be young or adult. And when I say learner I really mean all skiers as even experts still have lots to learn as the world whizzes by in a blur.

As a prime example, in fig 1 we can see a first-day beginner who, in the struggle to master basic technique, has become so tense that mastering any skill becomes impossible. At the same time the muscular stress has become extreme. Compare the beginner with the ski instructor in fig 2, and you can see how relaxed she looks even though she is moving at speed, exercising muscle control and performing technical skiing manoeuvres at the same time.

Learning to ski involves fitness, skill and motivation, but at the novice stage it is difficult to get the right balance between all three. As an aspect of fitness, flexibility and mobility are considerably more important for the beginner because, in acquiring the skills of skiing, muscular tension is by far the most common problem. Being tense will virtually halt the learning process, reduce motivation and will hurt. Starting off being flexible and mobile will reduce the effects of tension and promote a much steeper learning curve.

Intermediate

Ski equipment is so good these days that—with the proper instruction and guidance, on the kind of terrain that is not going to scare you out of your wits— progressing to the intermediate stage is a comparatively straightforward business. But, equally, this is where the problems can really start. The assumption that you've cracked it and can tackle anything can be a costly error of judgement. You have passed the awkward feeling of limb-punishing snow ploughs, but you will ski faster, longer, steeper and harder.

The term 'intermediate' is a bit of a misnomer because the level of competence that can be acquired by the beginner in a short time can quickly lead to them reaching the all-encompassing intermediate stage of learning to ski. A fortnight's holiday is enough to get well underway, but, unfortunately, not adequate to reach peak performance.

Here the problem is usually biting off more than you can chew, as progress is made ever nearer to more experienced stages. Encountering a black run strewn with moguls as big as a giant's staircase will reduce anyone's knees to jelly, except the best physically prepared.

Your fitness programme is always adding to your body's scope and mastering the techniques of skiing gives you a new skill. But here is the paradox for the intermediate going-on-advanced skier because getting better becomes a matter of reducing the amount of unnecessary body movements, and the more advanced modern ski

Fig 3: This skier is completely off balance.

Fig 4: **Despite his casual appearance, this skier is very stiff and his skis are crossed.**

equipment becomes, then the more important the balance mechanisms of skiing become.

In fig 3 this intermediate skier is near the top of a long downhill run, coming off a steep pitch. She is completely off balance, having over rotated. Fig 4 shows another skier in the same spot who looks casual but is in fact very stiff and, if you look closely at his skis, you will see that, as he tries to turn, he has, in fact, crossed his skis. Compare these two skiers once again to the ski instructor on page 10 and you can see the difference in poise and posture. So the intermediate still needs to exercise.

Advanced

Only when skiers have really got on top of controlling

their skis and found their perfect balance point, does pure fitness become a readily quantifiable element. It is no longer a question of compensating for bad technique, inconsistency and recurring mistakes. Being in balance on skis means effortless-looking skiing. Just look at the downhillers or slalom skiers at the winter Olympics, skiing in extreme conditions at the outer limits of their abilities. They feel the snow with their feet, tuning their bodies to sense the feedback coming from their high-speed environment. Seldom do they look to be stretched, but they have to train hard for 12 months when the races themselves last only seconds.

For expert and advanced skiers, fitness becomes a matter of choice because, as skiers get better, they exercise a whole variety of options concerning what kind of skiing they prefer. Some will search out wide open pistes for fast cruising, while others prefer tricky mogul-strewn runs and can turn on a sixpence. Steep powder or crusty slopes exert even greater demands and racing has its own very specific requirements.

In this area of ski fitness and preparation, it is much easier to decide how fit you want to be, the basic require-ment being the harder you want to push and the more challenges you seek, the fitter you will have to be. Anyone who contemplates any kind of ski touring should never consider any trip without first completing serious preparation well in advance.

The biggest problem for the expert is being lulled into a false sense of security by virtue of their good technique, which can mask lack of fitness. But, as with any skier, just getting started is the real problem. So get to it!

The division of labour

There is no doubt that someone who prepares for a particular sport derives much more fun, enjoyment, success and satisfaction from it than someone who doesn't. This is very true of skiing which, because of its dynamic nature, reflects the need for physical preparation to maximize participation.

The point here is to highlight methods of preparation to maximize safety, enjoyment and learning at whatever level you are, whether you are a beginner or an expert. For the first steps towards a fitness regime there is an important percentage split between general fitness and specific fitness for the different ski skills.

For the complete beginner 90 per cent general fitness should be the goal while specific fitness for skiing need only count for 10 per cent. Moving further up the mountain, and the ability scale, things equal out to 50–50, while at the top level the beginner ratio is reversed. Here general fitness should be maintained with a 10 per cent top up, but then specific ski fitness becomes more important.

What is fitness?

Generally speaking, 'total fitness' is a concept that involves every aspect of the individual—psychological and physiological. Physical fitness, with which we are primarily concerned here, forms a part of the whole concept and here the emphasis has been put on the elements that provide us with physical conditioning to create the best possible basis for you to become a better skier.

Physical fitness itself is made up of the following:

● **endurance** the ability to repeat a specific movement continuously for a period of time, such as walking, cycling, jogging

● **strength** the maximum force a muscle or muscle group can exert without concern for repeating the movement—for example in weight lifting

● **speed** the ability of the body working as a whole to respond quickly and efficiently, as when you just about catch the bus

● **flexibility** the range of movement at joint areas throughout the body, allowing ease of movement and control.

In terms of priority, different sports' disciplines would pick out different components as being the most important. The marathon runner, for example, needs more endurance than speed; the shot putter needs more strength than endurance, but, in the ski fitness programme, all the different levels have been borne in mind and you will find that some of all these elements have been incorporated.

Skiing requires a sound level of general fitness and, as you pass on from beginner/introductory levels, you will become more aware of the demands of the sport. Consequently, as already explained in percentage terms, your training becomes more specific, using exercises closely linked to skiing movements as well as maintaining general fitness.

To keep up any level of fitness you have established is no easy task, so avoid long lay-offs as these will quickly negate all your hard work. Also, having worked through a training programme you may lose motivation and find the whole thing tedious and boring. Keep your interest up by finding alternatives. Go jogging, try cycling or windsurfing, take a day off and go for a long walk or check out your local sports centre, get involved with another training programme or just change the tape in your personal stereo.

You and the training effect

Before you embark on a training programme consider the following, which will help to give direction and meaning to it as well as providing motivation and reinforcing your efforts.

Remember that first and foremost you are an individual with your various quirks and foibles. This is your starting point and how well you do will always relate to it. It is also important to consider other factors relating to yourself:

● **eating and drinking** try to establish a well-balanced diet, thus helping your body to respond to training more effectively

● **health** if you suffer from a medical condition or feel unwell as a result of training seek medical help *immediately*

● **recovery** rest properly after physical training, allowing your body to recover from strenuous exercise.

Having established your personal training programme it is important to allow your body time to adapt to the routine and the type of training you have decided upon.

The fitness effect

Your approach to physical fitness must be positive. To

exercise in a very comfortable manner will simply maintain existing levels of fitness. You must increase the actual output of your body in a controlled way before any 'fitness effect' occurs. This is called 'overload' which has three principles:

- **intensity**   the working load or effort per week

- **duration**   the amount of time in hours per week

- **frequency**   the number of sessions per week.

For example, the overload principle applied to jogging could be considered in the following way. As the programme develops, the intensity can be increased by running faster during each session, the duration by running for an extended period and doing it more often. Thus, using this concept, over a six-month period, the average person who started with a walk or a jog could run a marathon.

The approach to the development of your own physical fitness should initially be gentle but positive. A common mistake is to attempt too much too soon, which is demoralizing as well as damaging physically. Success in the early stages is important, both physically and mentally. Record your results each time you train and be aware of how you feel.

If you are a beginner, get the most out of skiing by remembering that, above all, active participation in the sport takes up a large part of the day in often hostile weather conditions. A good level of fitness can prepare the body for this situation and the strange, and at first, awkward equipment.

Try some of the exercises wearing your ski boots, particularly for the foot and leg rotations. Also, if enough space is available, try the same with your skis on, too. This will enable you to develop an awareness of the equipment in relation to the exercises.

Since the demands on the beginner are of a *general* physical nature, Circuit 1 of the exercises develops your general fitness to cope with these needs.

The intermediate/advanced skier, on the other hand, will be more familiar with the sport, recognize the importance of basic physical fitness and be seeking to practise a more specific regime. This is illustrated in Circuit 2, although embarking on the specific second circuit for stretching exercises without the grounding of the first is not recommended.

Work areas

Although it should be possible to work through any of the training schedules indoors in a relatively small room, work where you feel best. Perhaps in good weather extend the jog on the spot to outdoors, vary it if possible. Go jogging through woods or in a park, around trees, over logs. Adapt your programme to suit the facilities available.

Be ready, warm up

The body can often be compared to a machine where the best performance is achieved at working temperature.

The main priorities of the warm-up are, firstly, as security against injury by gently using and stretching the muscle groups, prior to harder work, secondly, to stimulate the heart and lungs to a ready state for harder work, and thirdly, to be ready for performance and participation.

As you work through the warm-up you will discover we are already developing areas of fitness, namely flexibility and endurance. Take your time and work through the sequence comfortably and methodically. You can put on some music if you like and then get started.

Warm-up

Stimulate circulation in the following ways:

JOG

Jog on the spot for 30 seconds

For 2 minutes, breathe gently, lightly and easily

Walk for 30 seconds

Repeat 30 seconds of jogging on the spot, but lift your knees higher until you touch your outstretched hands

Walk for 30 seconds

Repeat 30 seconds of jogging on the spot, lifting your knees to touch your fingers

Walk for 30 seconds

STRETCHING

Work through the joints of the body from the head down, and then back again

Take great care to establish a comfortable stretch by slow movements that could be held for at least 10 seconds, and don't forget to breathe!

Repeat stretches as part of the cool down period after circuits

HEAD ROLLS

Slowly circle your head so that
you feel a comfortable stretch
all round

Repeat 10 times in clockwise
and anticlockwise directions

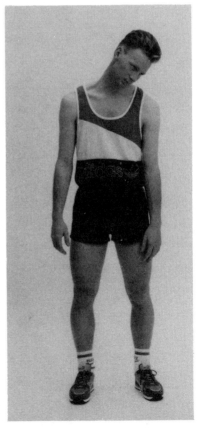

SHOULDER CIRCLES

Slowly make forward circles
with your shoulders, feeling
the stretch

Repeat 10 times backwards
and forwards

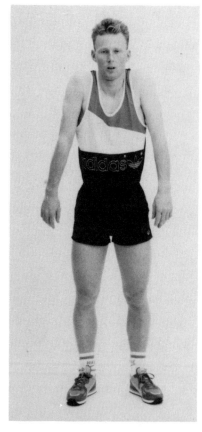

ARM CIRCLES

Make large forward circles with both arms

Repeat 10 times forwards and backwards

HIP CIRCLES

Trace a large imaginary hoop in the air with your hips, keeping your feet and head stationary

Repeat 10 times in both directions

COMBINATION STRETCH

Crouch down with your fingers on the floor in front of your feet

Keeping your head down, gently straighten your legs, feeling the stretch

Hold for 5 seconds

Walk your fingers up the front of your legs as your back unrolls, your head coming up last, finishing in an arched position

Gently reverse the sequence, rolling your head downwards towards the floor and repeat 5 times

UPPER BODY TWIST

Allow the momentum of your arms to carry your body round in the direction of the swing

Let your head follow the direction of the swing too, but keep your feet stationary

Repeat 10 times in either direction

LEG STRETCH

'Hug' your knee and gently pull it up towards your chest and hold for 10 seconds

Keep your eyes focussed on an object in front of you to help you balance

Repeat 5 times for each leg

LEG STRETCH 2

Grasp your foot and gently pull it backwards until you feel a stretch and hold for 10 seconds

Facing forwards again for balance, repeat 5 times for each leg

STRADDLE STRETCH

From the position shown opposite, gently stretch both hands forwards along your leg

Return to the sitting position then stretch your hands forwards between your legs

Return to the sitting position once again and repeat with your other leg

Repeat 5 times, holding each time for 5 seconds

FOOT ROTATIONS

Balance on one leg and rotate
your foot so that you feel a
stretch all round

Repeat 10 times with each foot

FURTHER EXERCISES

Now repeat the first, second and third exercises or, if you want to vary your routine, try skipping, open close hops and ankle flex hops using the same timing as given in the first exercise of the warm-up on page 23.

Skipping

Open close hops

Ankle flex hops

Circuit training

Having completed the warm-up it's now time to highlight the development of strength, speed and endurance. This is often best and most simply achieved by following a circuit that allows a slow build up, but also gives an excellent pay-off in the end. Don't waste time between warm-up and the circuit you are working through otherwise the benefits of the warm-up will be lost to you.

Circuit training is a very flexible system of exercising that utilizes a good variation to any programme. Once you start a circuit, however, take care to work through it carefully and to perform each exercise correctly—no cheating. It's best to do fewer repeats of each exercise rather than miss out exercises altogether.

The system set out in the following pages is referred to as 'relative dosage', the aim of which is to tailor any circuit to the individual using it. To give yourself the right dose, follow these simple rules:

● look through the exercises, running through them once or twice to feel what they are like, making sure you understand them

● now try each individual exercise for a period of one minute. Count your maximum continuous score (don't stop and start again). If you can't do any more *before* a minute is up, that's your maximum continuous score. Record your maximum score on the score sheet on page 64 in the 'M' column

● halve the score and enter the result under 'T', the training column, which will be your personal number of repetitions for each exercise

- Record the total time it has taken you to complete the circuit each time you try (it should decrease over three-week periods)

- Try to complete the circuit three times a week, say, Monday, Wednesday and Friday, keeping active on the other days

- Re-test your maximum scores after three weeks and don't forget that the circuit is continuous and involves three full repeats

KNEE TAPPING

Hold your hands in front of you
as shown below, and continuously jog on the spot, lifting
your knees high so that they
touch your hands

PRESS UPS

Start in the position shown below, resting on your toes, with your hands shoulder-width apart and your fingers pointing forwards

Lower and raise yourself, holding your body rigid and not touching the floor

If you score a maximum of less
than 10 use the chair method

TRUNK CURLS

Lying on your back, with your legs straight and together, raise your knees a few inches off the floor

Straighten your arms on top of your thighs and sit up to touch your knees with your hands

Lower yourself back to the floor slowly and make sure your hands stay on top of your legs at all times

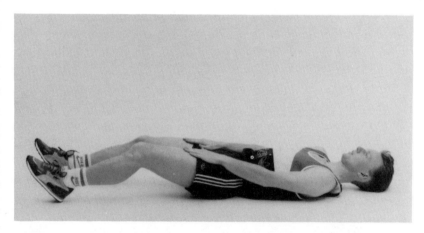

KNEE AND ANKLE FLEX

Keeping your feet flat on the floor, flex your knees and ankles and repeat

Imagine yourself on skis with your feet in the bindings

BACK ARCHES

Lying on your front interlock your hands under your forehead

Push yourself upwards on your hands and then slowly lower yourself back down to the floor

HOPPING

Place a strip or line on the floor and hop side to side

This is a fixed time exercise with 15 seconds for each leg

HEEL RAISES

From the starting position, raise yourself up onto your toes (notice the use of a thick book—you could substitute a block of wood if you prefer)

COOL DOWN (see page 56)

Circuit 2: Higher, faster, further

The second circuit is based on everything that has been done so far, but is aimed at more skilful skiers who are moving towards specific training. It is still important to maintain general fitness as this is the basis of the more specific second circuit.

Whether it is on a plastic slope or on actual snow during the winter, take advantage of every opportunity to ski. Think of working with and through a well-balanced, relaxed ski stance. If you play tennis or badminton you will be aware of how a relaxed ready position is far better for your game than is a tensed, stiff posture and the same principle applies to skiing.

BENCH BOUNCE

From a good ski stance, as shown below, pull up both feet sharply and land on top of a bench or box

Again retract both legs and land on the opposite side, then repeat

Establish dynamic continuous bouncing using your hands and arms to balance you

Try to keep your head level throughout

KNEE AND ANKLE FLEX

Using a firm support, concentrate on forming a good angulated position with your weight on one leg

Flex your knees forwards, keeping your heels on the floor,

and then return to the starting position

Repeat for both sides, recording your maximum on one leg to establish your circuit repetitions

TRUNK CURLS

Incorporate this exercise from
Circuit 1 (see page 42)

CROSS FLOOR BOUND

Place two markers approximately 8 feet (2.5 metres) apart

Start with one foot against the line, crossing the floor with a dynamic bound sideways towards the other line

Repeat, continuously and quickly, from side to side

HEEL RAISES

Incorporate this exercise from
Circuit 1 (see page 46)

HOP, TAP, RETURN

As with the bench bounce, use a bench or box, landing with your weight on the outside of your foot and, with your inside foot, tap on the floor

Repeat in the opposite direction, reversing your foot actions

Keep your body well centred and in balance

BACK ARCHES

Incorporate this exercise from
Circuit 1 (see page 44)

54

LEG SWING ROTATIONS

Concentrate on rotating your leg from the hip as you go through the forward part of the swing and repeat 15 times for each leg

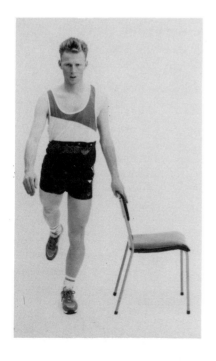 

Cooling down

Cooling down after exercise is very important. You must avoid stopping suddenly simply because the circuit has been completed. Continue to walk and stretch as highlighted during the warm-up phase and try to allow your body gently to return to a near-resting state. Cool down for about 10 minutes, enjoy a shower or bath and then relax.

Stretching

Stretching has become an important part of any programme. This is particularly true for ski racers but for really keen skiers generally it is an invaluable way to increase the body's flexibility. Stretching has been incorporated into many of the exercises so far but, to finish, here is a small simple programme.

LEG STRETCH

From a well-supported balancing position, swing your leg backwards and forwards to a comfortable stretch 15 times for each leg

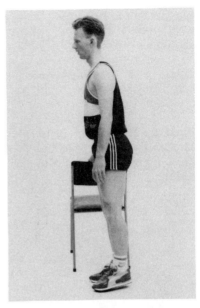

COMBINATION STRETCH

Lie flat on the floor, face down, with your hands under your shoulders

Relax your back and concentrate on keeping your hips on the floor

Push up until your arms are straight, allowing your back to arch, and then look up at the ceiling

Lift your hips into the air letting your head curl back as you do so and hold for 10 seconds

Return your hips to the floor, letting your head curl forwards as you do so with your arms still straight

Repeat 5 times

SNOWPLOUGH FLEXES

Stand with equal weight on both feet in the snowplough position

Flex both your ankles forwards

and then return to your starting position

Repeat 10 times

SNOWPLOUGH LUNGES

In the snowplough position, flex one knee forward to stretch your other leg

Repeat 5 times for each leg

SQUALK WALK

Walk sideways by starting with your heels together and toes apart, then moving your toes together and heels apart and so on so that you shift your whole body sideways

Repeat the heel toe movement 10 times to the right and then 10 times to the left

HEEL LIFT SWINGS

A development from the squalk walk but you keep your feet parallel, stretch up onto your toes as you turn

Repeat 10 times

GROIN STRETCH

In a sitting position, as illustrated below, apply pressure to the inside of your knees with your elbows

Feel the stretch and hold for 10 seconds

Repeat 5 times

Finally, go back to the very beginning before you go skiing. It's a good idea to do a brief warm-up in your room before you set out for the day's skiing. Also, before you take the first run, perform some simple stretching exercises with your skis on.

Getting fit and staying fit is the secret to skiing success. Blasting through knee-deep powder snow may *look* effortless when performed by the experts, but this or any other kind of skiing is not as easy as it looks. Learn as much as you can, push yourself within your limits and take on new challenges. Your potential relies on many things but none so important as fitness. Happy skiing!

Circuit table

EXERCISES	DATE:	Wk 1						Wk 2						Wk 3					
		M	T	t	T	t	T	t	T	t	T	t	T	t	T	t	T	t	M
1																			
2																			
3																			
4																			
5																			
6																			
7																			
8																			
9																			
10																			